Border Terriers

Illustrated by Jenny MacKendrick

First published 2015

The History Press
The Mill, Brimscombe Port
Stroud, Gloucestershire, GL5 2QG
www.thehistorypress.co.uk

Illustrations © Jenny MacKendrick, 2015

The right of Jenny MacKendrick to be identified as the Illustrator
of this work has been asserted in accordance with the
Copyright, Designs and Patents Act 1988.

British Library Cataloguing in Publication Data.
A catalogue record for this book is available from the
British Library.

ISBN 978 0 7509 6397 8

Design by The History Press
Printed in China

Border Terriers ...

are real honest dogs.

They're small and sturdy

and come in four different shades.

One of them's called grizzle.

They all have the same fearless nature,

independent spirit

and relentless attitude.

And they're all great kissers.

Border Terriers like ...

hunting,

digging

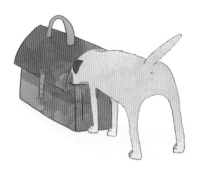

and exploring.

(They're really quite intrepid.)

They like chewing

and chasing,

jumping

and barking.

They love to play rough,

play dirty,

and play up,

especially if it's time to go home.

Border Terriers
need ...

a lot of walks,

a lot of supervision

and a lot of hosing down.

They need a secure home,

a secure garden,

an owner with a sense of humour,

consistent rules,

and a strong arm.

Border Terriers don't like ...

hot days,

boring days

or pamper days.

They don't like cats,

unless it's their cat.

And they don't like being shut in.

In fact, they can cross any wall ...

dig under any fence ...

and escape any fortress.

It just takes a bit of determination.

Border Terriers are ...

quick to learn,

slow to obey,

as hard as nails,

a bit of a handful,

always alert,

good tempered,

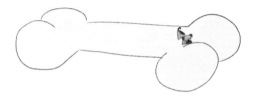

determined,

and loyal.

They're game for anything,

feisty,

persistent,

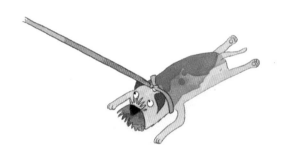

stubborn

and down to earth.

And they make great guard dogs.

Border Terriers have ...

rough coats,

short legs,

busy minds,

lots of energy,

an independent spirit,

a curious nature,

a comical face ...

and selective deafness.

Border Terriers will ...

drive you crazy,

work hard,

play hard,

fight hard

and love hard.

They'll jump up,

jump over,

be creative with obedience

and think for themselves.

They'll never let you go,

never let you down

and never be forgotten.

About the
Illustrator

Jenny MacKendrick studied drawing and applied arts at the University of the West of England. She now works as an artist and illustrator from her studio in Bristol, which she shares with Shona, her large and hairy Hungarian Wirehaired Vizsla, who is often to be found hiding under the desk.

Also in this Series
Labradors
Pugs
Springer Spaniels

www.thehistorypress.co.uk